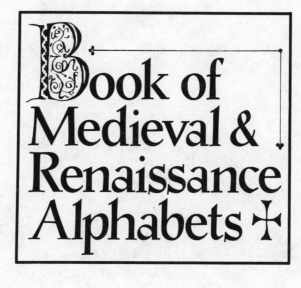

Book of Medieval & Renaissance Alphabets ✠

Book of Medieval & Renaissance Alphabets ✠

A Sterling/Main Street Book

Sterling Publishing Co., Inc.   New York

CIP Data Available

Text design by John Murphy

1 3 5 7 9 10 8 6 4 2

A Sterling / Main Street Book

Copyright © 1991 by Sterling Publishing Company, Inc.
Published by Sterling Publishing Company, Inc.
387 Park Avenue South, New York, N.Y. 10016
Distributed in Canada by Sterling Publishing
% Canadian Manda Group, P.O. Box 920, Station U
Toronto, Ontario, Canada M8Z 5P9
Distributed in Great Britain and Europe by Cassell PLC
Villiers House, 41/47 Strand, London WC2N 5JE, England
Distributed in Australia by Capricorn Ltd.
P.O. Box 665, Lane Cove, NSW 2066

Sterling ISBN 0-8069-8278-0

Contents

Introduction

Medieval and Renaissance Alphabets includes fifty-nine Latin alphabets, covering a wide range of lettering styles used over a period of ten centuries – from the 8th century through the 17th. The alphabets are arranged chronologically, and all are taken from original manuscript sources.

That the earliest of these alphabets appear to be missing three letters may be explained by reference to the history of the Latin alphabet. By the end of the first century A.D., the Latin alphabet was well established at twenty-three letters, lacking only the W and the differentiations of U from V and J from I. By the 10th century two variants of V were being used in writing: V at the beginning of a word and U in the middle. As time went by, the V-shape came to be used exclusively for the *v* sound and the U-shape for the *u* sound. In the 11th century, before the U-V problem was entirely solved, a need was felt for a symbol for the *w* sound, which had become common in a few languages, such as English. The solution was a double-V (VV) or double-U (UU), eventually written as W. In about the 15th century, J was differentiated from I. The J-form originated in a flourish to the left given to I when it appeared at the beginning of a word. J was placed after I in the alphabet, and its origin is still recalled by the dot over the lower case j and by the letter's Italian name – *I lungo*, or "Long I."

The close to sixty alphabets in this book reflect the complex evolution of minuscules (small letters) and majuscules (capital letters) during the thousand-year period between the Anglo-Saxon era and the late Renaissance. The modern English alphabet had of course developed from the Latin writing of the Romans, carried throughout the Continent and England by the Roman conquests and further spread by the growing influence of the Church and its scholarly communities. But it also reflects the influence of invasions and counter-invasions – both military and cultural – that followed in the wake of Imperial Rome's decline and fall. Consequently, the alphabets in this book reveal such diverse influences as the uncials of Anglo-Irish missionaries, the Caroline minuscule of learned Norman scribes, and the Gothic blackletters of German monks. Of these, the last proved immensely popular and spread throughout northwestern Europe, including England, from the 12th century through the 15th. Called blackletter because of their dark, heavy appearance, Gothic letters assume angular shapes due to the pen being held so as to make a slanting stroke. The rise and spread of Gothic letters is an excellent example of fashion at the expense of legibility. But many other alphabets within these pages are not only fashionable, but artistically unique. Still others anticipate Victorian and Art Nouveau alphabets by a thousand years.

The written word is the lifeline of our civilization. This wonderful gift of being able, by written symbols, to convey thoughts, not only to one another, but from generation to generation, has made possible our way of life, our law, our science, our literature, our graphic arts. Though fashions in lettering change from period to period, from age to age, the alphabets of the past are worth preserving for they find new uses in the present and help us to shape the future. Most of the fifty-nine alphabets in this book, representing the forward march of European civilization over ten centuries, cannot be found in any modern published source. They are all members of that happy domain called "public" and may be copied freely and frequently without begging anyone's permission.

Book of
Medieval &
Renaissance
Alphabets ✠

ABCDEFG

hihL ꟿN

ПBQRST

DUXM

ABCDEF
GHIJLM
NOPQRS
TUVV
XS

A A B C C D

E F G H H J L

G S S S S S T

C C D O H H N W

Q U Y Z Z

ABCDEF

GCHIJKL

MNNOPQ

RSTUVX

YZ.ÆM

AVA

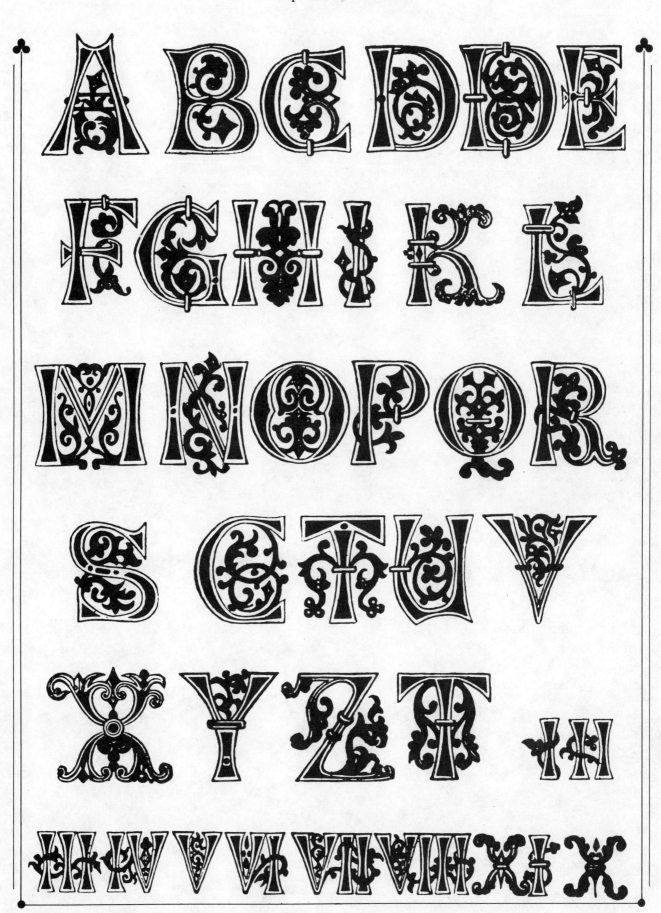

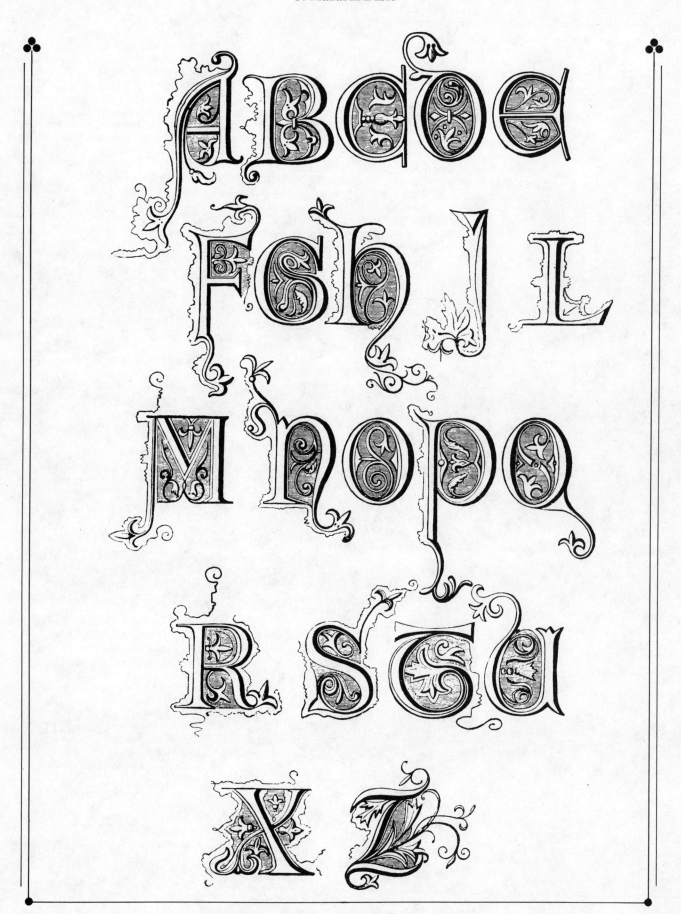

ABCDEF

GHIJKLM

NOPQRST

UVWX

YZ

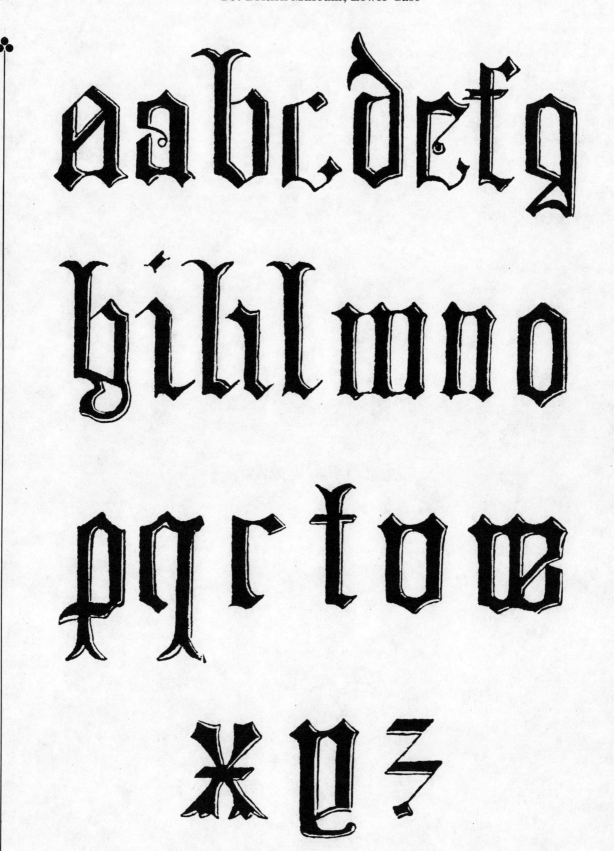

abcdefg

hiklmn

opqrst

vwxyz

ABADA

AGHIKL

MNOPOR

STUVW

ZNX

ABCD

DEFGh

IKLMN

OPQRS

TUVWX

YZTOZ

ABCDD
FGHIK
LMNOP
QRSTU
WXYZ

ABCDE
FGHIJ
KLMNO
PQRST
UVWXY
ƷYZƷ

ABCDEF

GHIKLM

NOPQRS

MUWX

YZ

ABCDE
FGHI KL
MNOPQR
ST ☩ TV
XYZ
☩ M

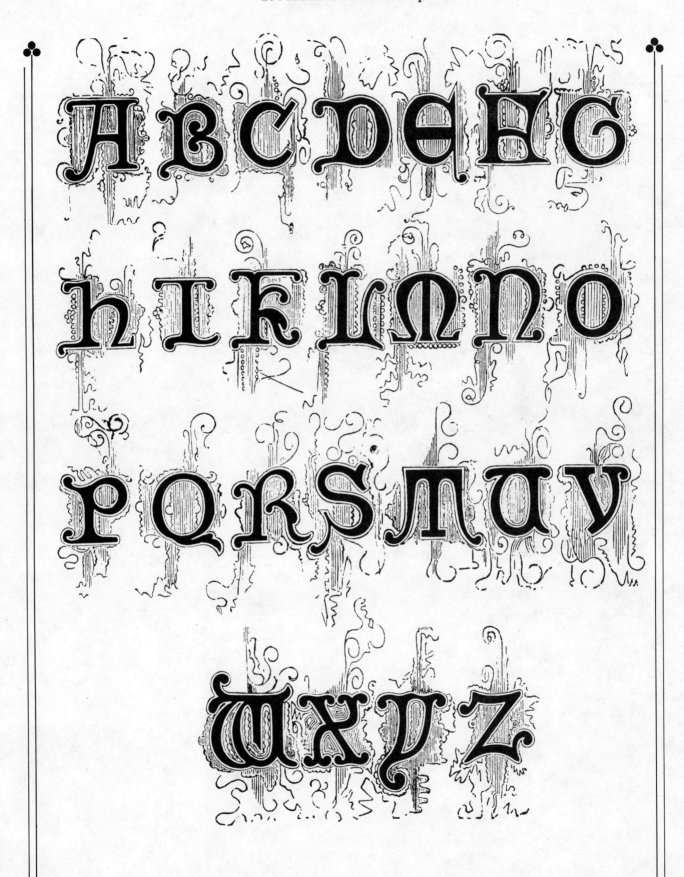

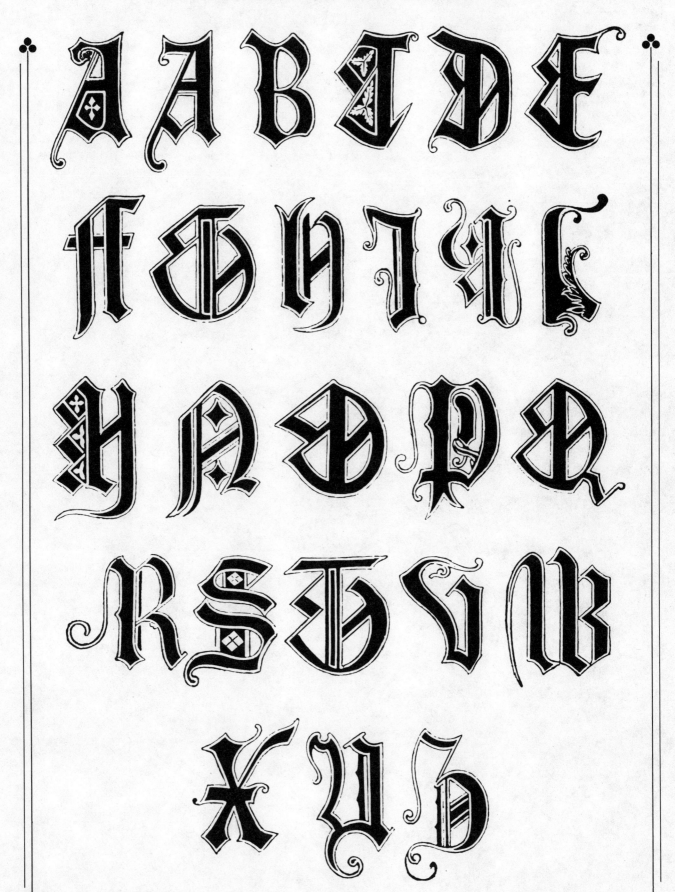

A B C D E

F G H I K L

M N O P Q

R S T U V

W X Y Z

A B C D
E F G H J
K L M N
O P Q R
S T U V
X Y Z

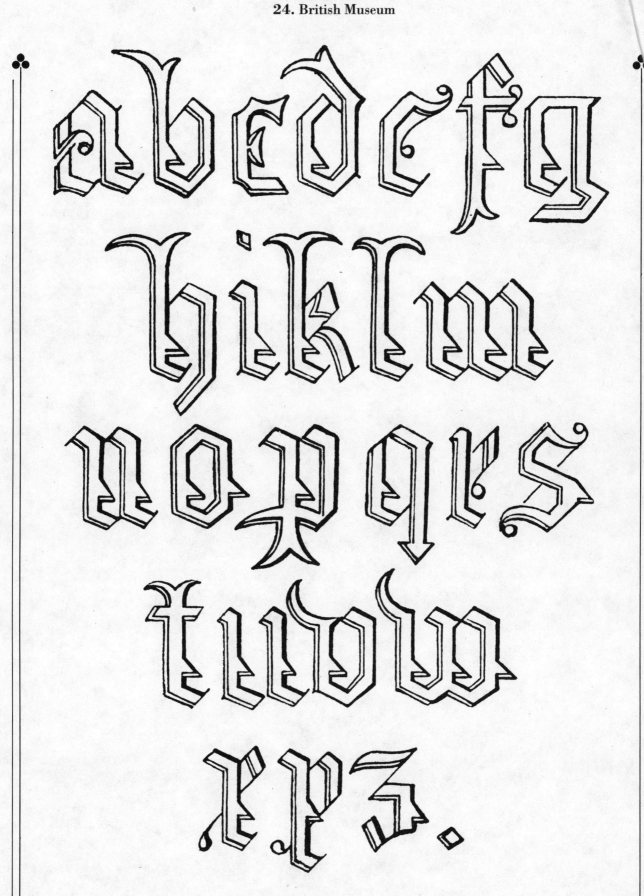

abcdefg

hiklmn

opqrstu

vwxyz.

ABCDE
FGHIK
LMNOP
QRSTU
XYZ

A B C D E

F G H I K

L M N O P

Q R S T U

W X Y Z

✠ ABC
D

DEFGH

KLMN

OPQR

STU

abcdefghi

klmnopq

r w s t v

v w x y z D

Aabcdef
ghijklmn
opqrst✠
uvwfyz&

ABCDEF

GHIKLM

NOPQR

STUVW

XYZ&E

aabcdefg

hijklmno

pqr stuv

wryz

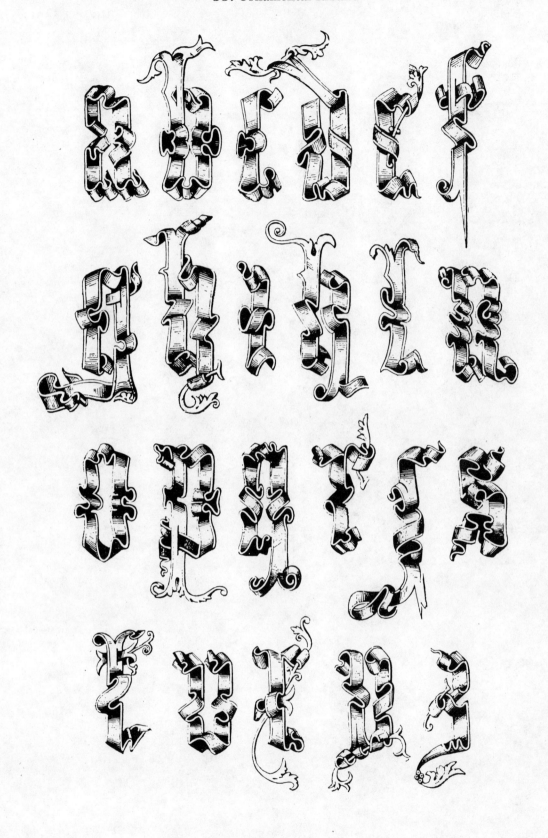

abcod

efghík

lmnopr

qstuv

xyz

ABCDE
FGHIJK
LMNOP
QRSTU
VWXYZ

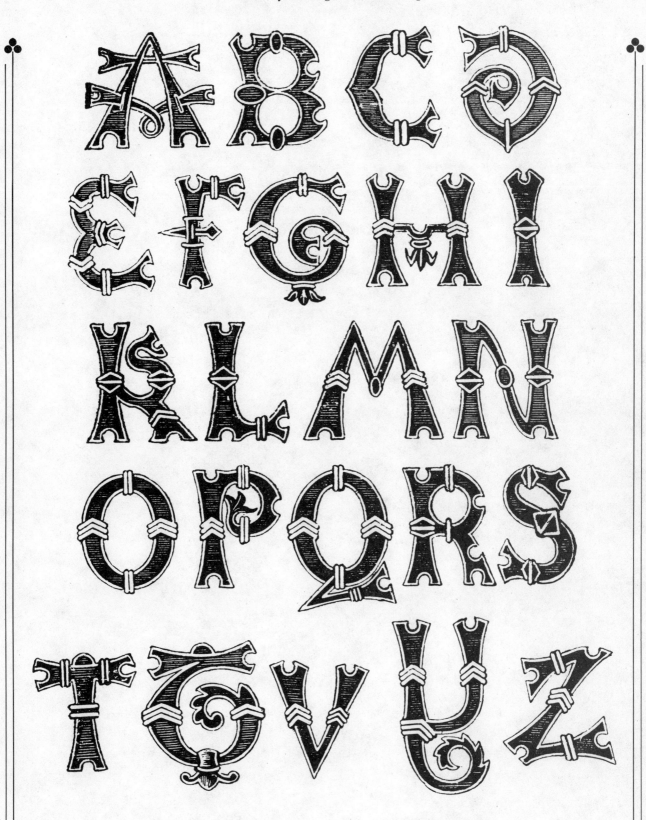

ABCDE

FGHIJK

ILMNO

PRSUT

UVWW

XYZ&

A B C D E

F G H I K L

M N O P Q

R S T U

V W X Y Z

abcdefg

hiklmnopq

rfsttuvwx

nzzz

ABCDE

FGHIKI

MNOPD

RSTUV

WXYZ

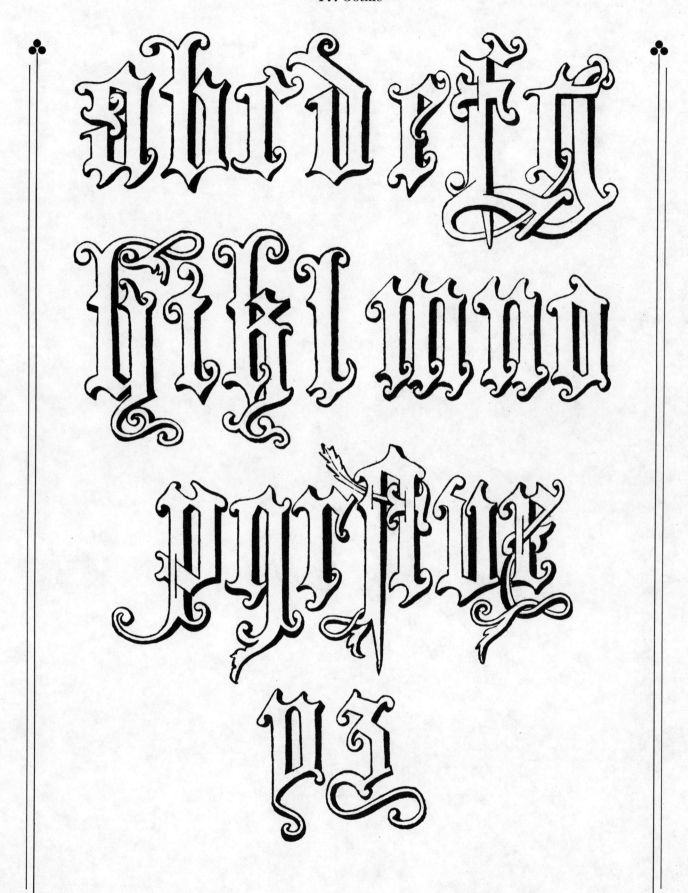

A B C D E
F G H I K
L M N O P
R S T U V
W X Y Z

A B C D E
F G H I K
L O V W T
A R S X U
V W X Y Z
1 2 3 4 5 6 7 8 9 0

abcdefg

hijklmn

onongrs

tuvxyzʒ

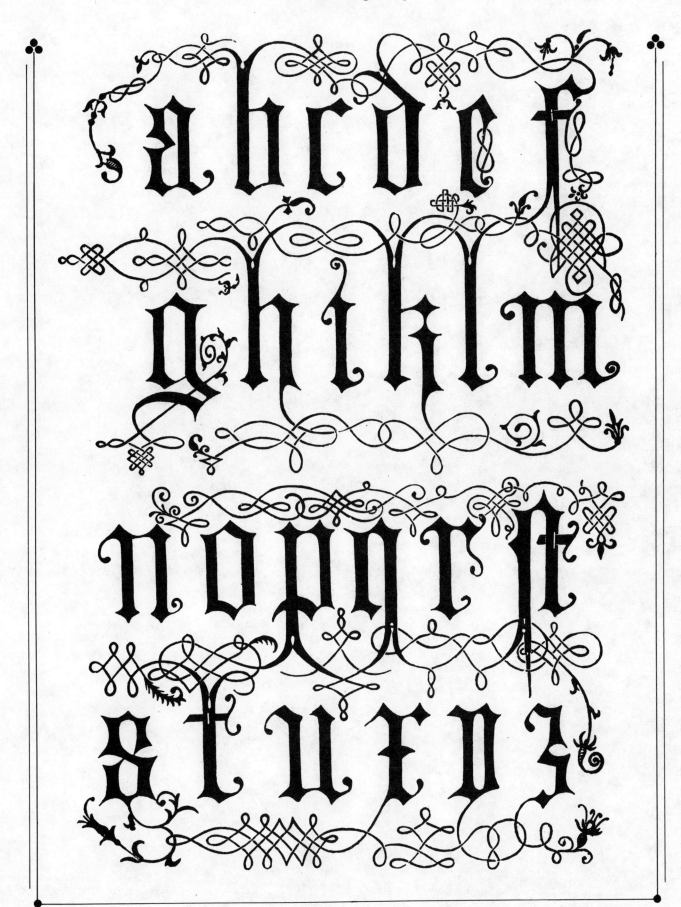

A B C D E
F G H I K
L M N O P
Q R S T U
V W X Y Z
1 2 3 4 5 6 7 8 9 0

abcdefgh

ijkl mnop

qrstu vw

xyz 1234

ABCDEF

GHIKLM

NOPQR

STUVW

XYZ

abcdefghij

klmnopqr

stuvwxyz

1234567890

ABCDE
FGHIJ
KLMNO
PQRST
UWY
ZX

ABCDEF
GHIJKL
MNOPQR
SSTUVW
XYZ

Index